DIARY OF A NATIONIST

The BON MOTS of JULIAN CASTOR

"Politics and a little bit of Pop"

Published by Forel Books
S. Pasadena, Florida
MMXI

Title Page Illustration:
AUBREY BEARDSLEY

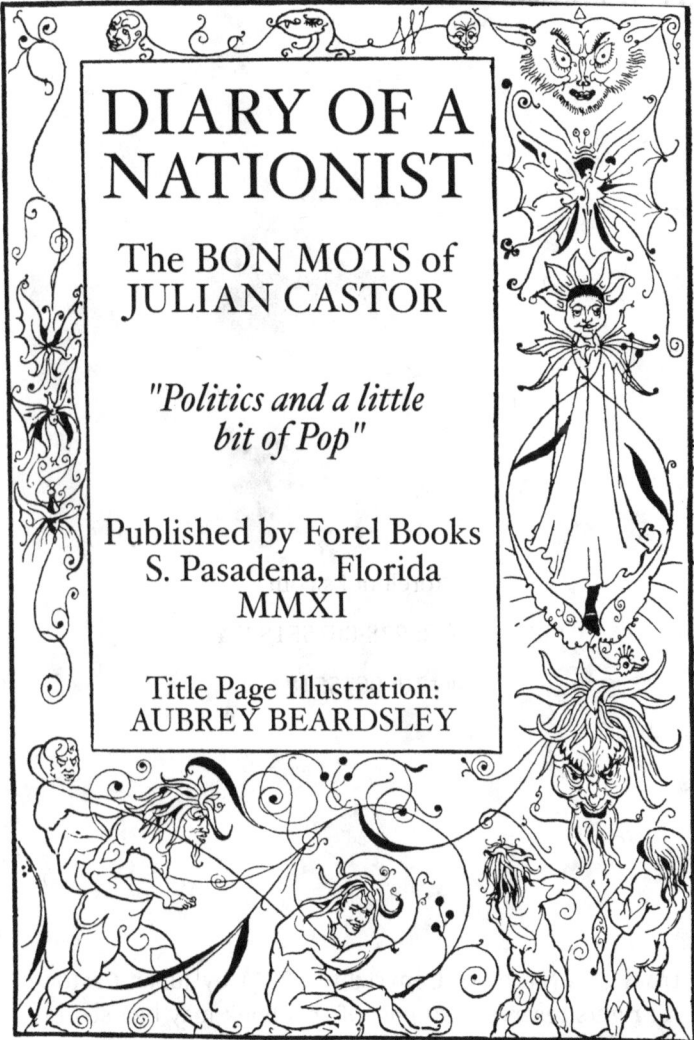

forelbooks.com

ISBN-13: 978-0615518374

ISBN-10: 0615518370

Of all the enemies to public liberty, war is, perhaps, the most to be dreaded because it comprises and develops the germ of every other. War is the parent of armies; from these proceed debts and taxes; and armies, and debts, and taxes are the known instruments for bringing the many under the domination of the few. In war, too, the discretionary power of the Executive is extended; its influence in dealing out offices, honors, and emoluments is multiplied; and all the means of seducing the minds, are added to those of subduing the force, of the people.

—James Madison

nationism *n. (Sociolinguistics)* The practical concerns of running a nation, especially seen as divorced from emotional beliefs about national identity. Contrasted with nationalism—*nationism* pertains to practical concerns, while *nationalism* pertains to questions of identity.

—Wiktionary

Our two-party system is a bowl of shit looking in the mirror at itself.

—Lewis Black

The national origin of a large corporation has no bearing on its actions. It doesn't necessarily care about its "nationality" at all, unless somehow it's in its interest to do so. Even back in WW2, certain "American" corporations (Ford Motors, IBM, etc.) did big business with Nazi Germany, which was against American interests. Today, if they can make more money by hiring overseas, that's what they do. It makes no difference whether stateside jobs get lost. Which makes sense because the purpose of corporations is to make profits for themselves, their owners and shareholders. Period.

***

The GOP's problem today is that it is really two parties: the Republican Party proper and the Tea Party. That they have coalesced is more a function of rhetoric's influence than of any actual political affinity: Tea Partyers in 2010 apparently believed the GOP's promises of "less taxes" and "smaller government." But the record shows that, in its own way, the GOP has often favored big, intrusive and expensive government (e.g. Patriot Act, Iraq and Afghanistan wars, expansion of Medicare, No Child Left Behind, Bush bailouts, War on Drugs, etc.). Thus, to a Tea Partyer, the GOP is just a pale shade more conservative than the Democratic Party—the lesser of two evils. This can not be the basis of an effective and unified political movement.

***

The world has changed, and so has America's place in it. When I was a kid, everything said "Made in USA" on it. Now it doesn't. Pretty much says it all.

In other words: Where are the jobs going to come from? A nation that doesn't manufacture isn't productive.

***

Republicans are the real communists.

Why do you think Republican states are called *red* states?

***

Assassinating Hugo Chavez would be a giveaway that we're scared of him. It would reveal a lack of self-confidence. Let him prattle on all he wants. Who cares? Would a lion kill a hummingbird? No, I say ... a thousand times *no!!*

***

The USA was never set up to be a Christian nation. That's clear. Most of the Founding Fathers were actually devoted Freemasons. Freemasonry contains Egyptian, Greek, Jewish, and Christian elements. The saying "In God We Trust" is all very well and good, but God is a universal spiritual concept and not the exclusive property of Christianity.

Of course, Christianity itself is a Jewish religion from the Middle East.

***

You can not simultaneously be a nationalist and a capitalist because, like communism, capitalism is international and aspires to be global. It wants it all. Communism would accomplish its goals by exporting revolution from one country to another, capitalism by having the big banks and corporations spread their business everywhere. The logical end-result of each system is a one-world order—a global political-financial monopoly with no boundaries. That would indicate total success on its part. Fascism was originally an attempt to transcend this dialectic by offering a third, nationalist path.

***

First of all, let's get one thing straight: the USA is *not* a democracy because the people for the most part do not decide any policy—the politicians do. The USA is a republic. The people ("We the People of the United States of America ...") merely vote on which politicians get to govern us.

If this country was a democracy, there'd be less politicians and less need for them. All issues, policies, and laws would get decided by referendums and plebiscites.

Everything held to a popular vote—that would be a democracy.

***

Democrat—One who'd rather be a slave to big government than to big business.

Republican—One who'd rather be a slave to big business than to big government.

***

"Republicans are real Americans."

See, now that right there is an un-American thing to say.

Liberals love their country. They just don't get all patriotic about it because they know that patriotism is used by politicians to emotionally manipulate the citizenry. Oldest trick in the book.

***

Since McCain-Palin lost the election in 2008, the political rhetoric has been increasingly brutal and crass.

***

Dictatorships come in all political stripes: communist (Stalin, Mao, Castro), capitalist (Shah of Iran, Pinochet, Mubarak), and fascist (Mussolini, Hitler, Perón).

***

I'd say that, as a whole, the Founding Fathers were mainly concerned with two things: the undue influence of big government and of big business.

***

It's interesting to note that, from antiquity to now, the reign of the world's leading nation (superpower) has gotten shorter and shorter. Ancient Egypt's tenure lasted several thousand years. The Roman Empire's was several hundred years. The British Empire's was a couple centuries. The USA's was almost a century. China's may be over almost before it began. From a broader historical perspective, China may simply be fulfilling the brief role assigned to it by this "telescoping of time."

***

One problem with racism is that it's an incredibly lazy way of thinking.

"All people of this race are just like this ..."

It works from generalizations and the supposed law of averages, but doesn't recognize exceptions or the uniqueness of individuals.

If you let go of your racism, then you have to assess each person you come across based on his or her own qualities. And no more "free pass" for those of races you like. Sure, it's more work but work is good for you. It's like exercise for your mind and keeps you on your toes.

***

What happens is that liberals and conservatives have each created their own "reality maps" based on contrary interpretations of the facts.

Each side is sincerely convinced that what it "knows" is the absolute truth.

But, as the old saw goes, the truth is somewhere in the middle.

***

The GOP made its bed with the Tea Party and

now it has to lie in it.

Which sounds great, except come November 2012.

***

In the USA, and much of the world, the problem at heart isn't big government but big business (large banks and corporations).

The reason is simply that government is itself unofficially (off the books) run by big business. You see evidence of this on many levels: from campaign contributions to special-interest lobbying to the revolving door of big business bosses "serving" at the highest levels of government. Then there is the question of the Federal Reserve Bank—actually a series of twelve private banks—which creates the money that the Treasury Department prints. I'd agree that whoever controls money controls the system. For what can a government do without money? Regimes, dynasties, and entire nations rise and fall because of money.

This is why government is knee-capped and often doesn't represent the interests of the people (as indicated in the Bill of Rights and Constitution). We the People have violated the Constitution—allowed it to be violated—and have to pay the price.

***

I think the current Iranian regime is pretty horrible, but the Western powers have a problem: they want to stop Iran from having something they themselves have (nuclear weapons). The hypocrisy is astounding, and of course no one questions it.

This double-standard is at the root of the moral weakness of their position.

The United States is, to date, the only country that has ever used nuclear weaponry on an enemy. And it's done so twice. And both times on civilian populations.

The question also remains: does any nation or global organization have a right to tell a sovereign nation what it can and can not do with its own government, industry, economy, etc.?

***

The Decider is not pleased with Scott McCtellin.

***

If Israel still needs our financial aid after all these years, then something is wrong.

***

Many GOPers' perception of reality is interesting—it involves forgetting what occurred from 2000 to 2008.

***

Barack Obama is the first half-white President of the United States.

***

Moneyism (more commonly known as capitalism) is the system in which banks and corporations are dominant. In such a system, society naturally becomes imbued with the values of banks and corporations, which by necessity are materialistic and monetary. Then everything is a commodity and has a price: we speak of "how much money a person is worth," land becomes "real estate," unique objects are "collectible," homes are "properties," nature is "exploitable," the people are "consumers" who are classified into "markets," and persons are judged by their "credit ratings."

***

credit *n.* The opportunity to get into debt: *Tom's credit score is higher now, so he can borrow more money (i.e. incur more debt).*

***

I always suspected George W. Bush is a foreigner—he doesn't speak English very well.

***

Sarah Palin is like a cross between Eva Mendes and Dan Quayle.

***

Ever notice how the side you're on always happens to be the good side?

And the side you're against happens to be the bad one?

Works that way every time. Even when you change sides.

***

What's odd is that Mubarak looks exactly like a cross between Ronald Reagan and Hugo Chavez.

***

Frankly, I'm very disappointed in the Tea Party militias. They could have snazzy uniforms but don't. No sense of paramilitary style whatsoever.

***

Not every culture likes Western-style "total" freedom because in such freedom there are too many possibilities and options to choose from. But when freedoms and choices are more limited, it's easier and more streamlined (for some) to function and they then actually feel more free, not less.

***

USA support for Israel is a holdover from the Cold War mentality.

Israel is a tiny country—one-seventh the size of Florida.

Personally, I sympathize with Israel but recognize it's not in the USA's interests to support it because it automatically engenders the opposition of much of the official Muslim world—a mass of countries ranging from North Africa to the Middle East all the way to Southeast Asia.

***

The problem with "intelligent design" is its built-in anti-evolution agenda. Otherwise it could just be pantheism—the doctrine that God is everywhere.

***

My view is that the universe is the aspect of God that is perceivable by our five senses. It's the physical body of God, so to speak.

***

God may be another way of saying "existence" or "the intelligence behind existence."

If we're intelligent, the universe must be as well since we're just another product of the universe. It was here first.

To say the universe isn't intelligent and that we were created by chance is like saying you can take a bunch of raw minerals, metal ores and chemical compounds, throw them into a massive blender, and expect a jet airliner to come out.

***

I think most Republicans would openly admit there is no GOP plan for jobs other than to "step aside and let the free market do its thing." Competition, capitalism, and such.

Small-government ideology, you see. Unless by "federal government" you mean the Department of Defense and armed forces. In that case, it's big-government ideology. (Which is funny, considering that, throughout history, armies have been the main tool of tyrants.)

"Competition will correct the market," they say. But they don't seem to consider that, in a pure and unregulated free market, businesses and corporations soon form cartels and trusts, and thereby eliminate true competition.

***

Doesn't matter if we find a presidential candidate we can trust. If he wins, he'll turn into a president we can't trust.

And it won't necessarily be his fault. The system is absolutely crushing.

***

"Real American ... true American." You're an American if you're born, or naturalized, in the USA. That's all. What, you may ask, is the USA? Why, it's the land which the US federal government has jurisdiction over.

***

Mubarak seems like he's willing to let Egyptians kill each other in the streets so that he can be president for another seven months.

This is after his already being president for thirty years.

What's wrong with this picture?

***

In our two-party system, maybe both sides stink. Maybe sometimes "My enemy's enemy is still my enemy."

***

Blaming Jews or Americans or Arabs as a whole—or any other group—for the world's problems is ultra-lame.

Talk about adolescent attempts to avoid responsibility.

You have to blame individuals who literally and personally cause trouble, not the ethnic groups to which they belong!

***

The White Stripes were/are a great band.

I can't help thinking it's kind of weak for them to break up. It's like they're afraid to continue and "not be that good any more." But if Jack White can't be that "good" with Meg any more, why would he be that good with other bands?

Suddenly, he seems less interesting as an artist. Maybe it's because what made him cool was the dialogue he had between the White Stripes constant and all these other bands. Now it's just the other bands or the ("shudder") solo career.

While Dead Weather and Raconteurs are really cool, they just don't have the simplicity, humor, and brilliance of the White Stripes.

***

Banking is a tradition that started when money was physically cumbersome—either sacks of gold or, later, paper bills. You needed someone to store it and guard it for you.

Now it's electronic digits.

It's a big secret that banking is no longer necessary.

A bank makes a lot of money off your money. I mean that literally. Banks are allowed to make money out of thin air to the tune of nine times their actual deposits. They loan this money they've declared and make interest off it—not to mention get paid the principal. Remember that we're talking about electronic digits here.

***

In his new book, Donald Rumsfeld says that, even if he had known Saddam had no WMD, he still would have invaded Iraq. I believe him—since that's exactly what happened anyway.

Darnold Rumspilled—who you kidding, dude?

I myself knew that Saddam didn't have WMD, so you definitely knew.

***

Conservative/liberal is like saying past/future.

***

The big industrial infrastructure corporations

like Halliburton are a big part of the capitalist bloc which uses the US government as its face. They have helped corrupt, ravage, and indebt many of the third-world nations by coercing them to accept massive building and development projects they don't need and can't afford. For these poor countries, Halliburton and Bechtel are WMC (Weapons of Mass Construction).

***

Okay, so the day comes when there's a global political monopoly—a one-world government. It rules the world.
Then what?
Big power = Big headaches
LOL

***

Everything Obama says is a lie. For instance, his real name is Barnard José O'Banner and he was born in Sweden.

***

I agree the Second Amendment (the right to bear arms) was designed to prevent tyranny. I used to think it was bullshit that an armed citizenry could ever check government power and be a match for the strength of the US Armed Forces. Until I saw what happened in Iraq, where a bunch of ragtag insurgents gave the US military a real headache for years on end.

***

2011 is the year that Sarah Palin poops or gets off the pot. She either begins campaigning for president or she does not.

Either way, this is going to be a predicament for Sarah.

If she doesn't run, she's going to disappoint a lot of her supporters who consider a run for the White House the whole point of supporting her.

But if she does run, she's almost certainly going to lose the GOP nomination, which will eliminate her viability as a politician.

Much of her present power is based on the vagueness of what her future path is ... is she a political heavyweight or merely another talking head? A vagueness which is about to get cleared up, one way or another.

***

It's interesting to see how the Republican Party has built up the Ronald Reagan myth. He's given credit for big things he didn't really accomplish (mainly, the breakup of the Soviet Union). But Reagan is the only possible Republican president who could be an idol for the GOP. Who else would fit? Eisenhower? Too remote in time. Nixon? Too uncharismatic and disgraced. Ford? Too bland and inconsequential. Bush Sr.? One-termer. George W. Bush? Too close in time and unpopular. So, by default, it's Reagan who gets the mythical makeover. The myth describes Reagan in roughly the same way that *Happy Days* authentically captures the '50s.

***

Beyond a certain level of sophistication, technology becomes the enemy of employment. It can then do more things and do them better, more quickly and more cheaply than before. The problem we face today is the one-two punch of rapidly developing technology and population growth.

***

During George W. Bush's administration, many liberals tended to compare him with Hitler. I always thought this was absurd. In the first place, Hitler was a brilliant orator, whereas Bush could barely enunciate a coherent thought. Second, Hitler was a self-made man who came from a humble background, whereas Bush was a daddy's boy from an elite family who coasted through life on the strength of his family name. And, third, Hitler actually saw extensive combat in WW1 and earned the Iron Cross, First Class (one of Germany's highest decorations), whereas Bush spent the Vietnam War partying in Alabama while assigned to a cushy national guard unit. There are other differences (Hitler wore a Nazi Party pin, Bush a US flag pin; Hitler was known as the Führer (Leader), Bush as the Decider, etc.) but I think the point is made.

***

In the US, Democrats and Republicans in effect function as the left and right wings, respectively, of the same party. Deep down inside, and behind closed doors, the leaders are best buddies. They trade power back and forth for decades on end (and counting). All the passionate and brutal disagreements between them are clever "hot button" issues designed to make drama and rile up their bases (i.e. the proles): taxes, abortion, gay marriage, healthcare, gun rights, and so on. They need to keep it interesting and have the citizens emotionally invested: this keeps the cherished donations and votes coming in. It's moronic but works wonders for the politicians' careers.

***

American politics is a non-athletic spectator

sport of two teams. The fans root for their team, and jeer the rival team, no matter what. And some of the commentators even pretend to be neutral.

***

Ann Coulter and Hillary Clinton are both blonde strong-willed women who are considered sexually repulsive by men of the opposite political tendency.

***

I'll admit that Sarah Palin is an attractive and good-looking woman. However, that of itself does not qualify her for high office. I don't want her being president of the United States. I also don't want her performing surgery on me, piloting a jet airliner I'm traveling on, or building my home.

***

I can relate to the conservative view on abortion. What makes me suspicious is that conservatives who, for everything else, are incredibly hard-ass and severe, suddenly become fountains of hyper-sensitivity and empathy when the subject of an embryo or fetus, or even some cells, comes up.

***

On abortion, liberals often protest that women should be allowed to do what they want with their own bodies. I suspect that conservatives don't care what women do with their own bodies so much as with the body of the unborn child. "After you give birth and the child is safe, go jump off a bridge if you want."

***

Abortion is a complex issue. But what it comes down to is the question of when life begins. Conservatives work with the premise that life begins at conception, liberals that it begins at birth (or, in many views, after the first trimester). I submit that we don't actually know when life begins and so either view is plausible. It may be that, the moment the zygote is created, there is a person there, albeit in a very primitive form. On the other hand, it may be that, all through gestation, the developing embryo/fetus, though biologically alive, is really more an organ or extension of the mother and only becomes a person when he or she is born: perhaps, as the ancients believed, the soul (or person's essence) enters the body with the first breath taken … and leaves with the last breath. And everything in between those two breaths is what we call "life."

***

Ironically, conservatives as a rule sound more left-brain (linear, analytical) and liberals more right-brain (holistic, creative).

***

I'd like to clear up a vast misconception. The Republican Party of today is, for the most part, not really conservative. It is neo-conservative, which I'd define as big-government conservative. This explains why our government is so bloated and stagnant—it's made up of liberals and pseudo-liberals slugging it out in a crazy love-hate fest. It's pretty incestuous, which is a fancy word for in-breeding. The real conservatives are the Libertarian Party, which unfortunately has little to no political power.

***

I'm hoping Sarah Palin will eventually get the GOP nomination. And that her running mate will be Christine O'Donnell.

That would rule.

Especially if, at some point during the campaign, the two have a televised jello wrestling match, like just to have some fun and let off some steam.

***

The working class has one thing the elite class

doesn't have: numbers. As in many numbers of votes. They have tremendous power but, not being united, don't use it.

If someone could harness that power intelligently and wisely, it'd be an impressive force.

I believe someone once said: *E Pluribus Unum* ("Out of the Many, One").

***

Lenin. Stalin. Palin.
I think I'm seeing a pattern here.

***

I don't know why the USA always has this compulsion to meddle in the affairs of other countries. It's like a guy who wants to have four wives. Four times the headaches!

Could it be compensation for an insecurity? You'd think that wouldn't be possible, with everything the USA has accomplished. It's like a woman who's a top fashion model but thinks she's fat so she convinces her homely sisters to eat more than they should.

***

Republicans strongly oppose gun control and promote the people's right to bear arms because they (reasonably) believe it's an effective check on government tyranny. Yet they also promote massive spending for the military, which is the main force that the government would use to enforce tyranny. It's as though both sides are (unwittingly?) being primed for some massive showdown.

***

Why is it that the only members of the George W. Bush administration who I found to be at all humanistic were Condaleeza Rice and Colin Powell?

***

Twenty-year-old Bristol Palin, unwed mom since she was a teenager, is an advocate for unwed teen sexual abstinence.

That's kind of silly, isn't it?

***

The word "conspiracy" has gotten thrown around a lot, especially since 9/11 happened. Such an ominous and sinister-sounding word!

But, for those involved on the inside, it's just business as usual: promoting their interests and agendas, and covering their behinds.

As simple and as complicated as that.

***

The people always have the real power. But they rarely harness it or apply it.

But, even though it sounds corny, in union there is strength.

Just imagine if, instead of the USA being one nation of fifty states, there were instead fifty separate little nations. Think it would have the same power it has now?

***

By definition, centrists are the most balanced along the political spectrum.

Leftists and right-wingers each defend their ideologies and view the world through them.

But a centrist usually asks, "Personal ideologies aside, what's the problem and how can it best be solved?"

***

The USA was founded as a revolutionary nation. But yesterday's revolutionary often has a way of becoming today's reactionary.

***

The problem with our Afghan military strategy

is that we even have one.

We should be out of there yesterday.

***

The lamestream media ignores Ron Paul.

Which is a shame because he seems the most intelligent, ethical and capable of the Republican hopefuls.

Even so, his libertarian philosophy would have a hard time if it had to deal with the politico-economic status quo.

Unless the economy had totally tanked by then.

***

The War on Drugs has got to be considered a massive failure in every sense. It has lost billions of dollars with no discernible benefit to the people of the United States of America. Not only has it not achieved its stated goal (reduction of illicit drug use) but the precise opposite has occurred. Why is a policy that is so ineffective continually implemented anyway? Millions of Americans have been imprisoned for possessing, buying, or selling legislatively disapproved drugs—essentially for engaging in commerce or personal consumption. I'm pretty confident we can do better.

***

Although vice—drugs, gambling, prostitution—has often been criminalized, at heart it is just a public health issue. More on a par with, say, obesity, occupational safety, and accident prevention than with murder, rape, and kidnapping. Penalizing vice violates the principle of self-liberty, which is the right to do things to yourself or with your own body, even if potentially unhealthy and/or unsafe. There are many legal activities that are unhealthy and/or unsafe, such as motorcycle riding, bungee jumping, and being overweight. One has to really sit and wonder why these have not been criminalized yet.

***

So far, Congress has decided to continue supporting organized crime and overburdening the police and courts by waging the War on Drugs. Maybe some day all drugs will have the exact same legal status as alcohol—minimum age of 21 for users, can't drive under the influence, and so forth. And maybe all vice will be legal for consenting adults.

***

The logic of the Drug War goes something like this: We care about you and don't want you to do something unhealthy (drugs). But if you do this unhealthy thing, we will take away your freedom and put you in prison (a dangerous and unhealthy environment). Because we care about you.

***

Israel's tragedy is its location, smack dab in the middle of the Arab world. Obviously, the Jewish people deserve their own nation. All their troubles since the Diaspora revolved around the fact that they were stateless: perpetual guests in host countries, they were variously viewed as parasites, infiltrators, or subversives. Holding on to their own particular identity, their assimilation could never be complete. A united people defined by a lack of statehood may feel equally at home in every state and thus be mistrusted and abused by each state.

But the formation of its own state in 1948 has not brought Israel peace. It is in fact consigned to a permanent war footing. There is no solution to the Israeli-Palestinian conflict. Even if an official accord was reached, a fanatic on either side could set a bomb off and the conflict would restart.

Most considerations surrounding this land are highly emotional, not rational. This is completely due to its location, a land where the Big Three Religions intersect. Picked by religious Zionists for its Biblical history. What if, instead, secular Zionists had come forth and swayed the course of events? I can still envision Jews of the world uniting to legally purchase a tract of land—larger and more fertile than Israel's—in a third-world country that would welcome the cash and the opportunity to have a thriving, developing nation on its new border, say somewhere in South America or Africa. What if Israel were a "state of mind" and could be located elsewhere? In the same way that European civilization was able to thrive transferred to the wilderness of the New World. A second Israel or a new Judea.

***

On some level, the Tea Party has intuited that the GOP is not what it says it is. For instance, for all its anti-tax rhetoric, the GOP has never made any effort to repeal the Sixteenth Amendment (federal income tax). Why is that?

Even though the GOP routinely pays earnest lip service to Reagan's famous quip ("The nine most terrifying words in the English language are, 'I'm from the government and I'm here to help.'"), the federal government has steadily grown and gotten more expensive and authoritative during Republican administrations. "Small government" has come to merely mean "little to no regulation over business." But when it's time for government to do business with, or fund, private corporations, it can never be too big.

The Tea Party's partial identification with the GOP may indicate it is confused by the conservative-like talk. After all, Tea Partyers are mostly idealistic novices while the GOP is—just like the Dems—made up mainly of experienced career politicians.

But at least Dems are consistent: they *admit* they're for big government.

***

The main dysfunction of the Democratic Party is its ideology of social enabling. Enabling can be described as "maintaining a person's self-defeating traits by preventing him or her from experiencing the consequences of his or her actions." What makes enabling so insidious and disarming is that it's not malicious: it's usually accompanied by all kinds of high-minded and sympathetic intentions. Yes, it's definitely better than outright malice. However, that's not exactly a standard to be proud of. I agree the elderly should be able to retire in comfort and security. I also agree there should be a modest government safety net—but it shouldn't turn into a trap.

***

At its core, the Republican Party has a need to be duplicitous toward its own members; by this I mean that, if it wants to survive, it can not openly enunciate its agenda in any clear way. It must resort to window-dressing it with what it deems are noble concepts.

Its core agenda is very simple: government should continually support the private banking/corporate sector and never interfere with it in any way that causes it undesirable expense. This agenda is utterly self-centered. It can only benefit, at most, a few thousand citizens, and, if nakedly stated, the GOP would likely never win a single election. So the erection of a broad ideology begins ... protecting small business owners ... pro-life ... family values ... gun rights ... condemning gay marriage ... anti-immigration ... patriotism ... "don't ask, don't tell" ... faith-based initiatives ... anti-intellectualism....

***

More than being an accurate record of past events, history acts as the mythology of humanity's past. Both winners and losers write the history books, but it's the winners' books that get read (losers have less resources and credibility).

***

Even if China becomes the next world super-power, I doubt it will ever be "another America." So far, the only thing it's offering is cheap manufacturing and economic efficiency. Where are the ideals that stir people's imaginations? The USA, with its ethnic multiplicity, pioneering opportunities, economic magnitude, freedom of expression, unbridled creativity, and dynamic action, has been a beacon to the world. Even if the American myth was not completely true, it was true enough. It rang out and resonated with much of the world. China will have to change radically to achieve anything comparable—but, being such an ancient country, how feasible is that?

***

Hitler's sin was that he tried to accomplish in the 20th century what the United States accomplished in the 19th. Where the Third Reich expanded toward the East, the USA expanded toward the West. Where the Third Reich had the rallying mission word *"Lebensraum"* (living space), the USA had "Manifest Destiny." Where the Third Reich committed genocide against Jews, Gypsies and Communists, the USA committed genocide against Native Americans. Where the Third Reich had death marches, the USA had the Trail of Tears. The main difference between the two is one of scale: by Hitler's time, industrial and communications technology had developed significantly so that the number of victims could rapidly be multiplied many times over. It also meant that the details of the process could be recorded photographically; our knowledge of Nazi atrocities is thus much more vivid. The second difference, of course, is that the Third Reich lost.

***

Growing up, as a kid and teenager, these presidents—some before my time—seemed noble and gave me "good vibes": Roosevelt, Truman, Eisenhower, Kennedy, and Carter; and these seemed creepy and gave me "bad vibes": Johnson, Nixon, and Reagan.

Later on, I found both George Bush (Sr.) and Bill Clinton acceptable. It always seemed like an affectation when people got too worked up over them.

***

Remember when, in the Bush-Cheney years, the administration's supporters would substitute the word "freedom" for "French" to demonstrate their anger at France's disagreement over Iraq? People ordered "freedom fries," "freedom kissed," and "freedom-inhaled" cigarettes. After a while I began thinking, "Man, the French must really be a free people."

***

The meat, poultry, and dairy industries for the most part are needlessly vile and atrocious.

Animals should not have to go through Auschwitz for us to eat. In many other countries, clean free-range living and a quick death are routine. And when you eat in those countries, the food tastes more and better. Ultimately, whose food is it anyway, ours or the industries'? If we're paying for it, doesn't it then become our food?

***

Doing away with compulsory military service has, in some respects, been a disservice to the nation's social and emotional fabric.

It acted as a rite of passage: for at least one year, a young man had to live in close quarters with others, work in a spirit of teamwork, be disciplined, learn certain skills, and get physically fit.

Also, the general population's participation in the military is much closer in spirit to the Founding Fathers' doctrine of having citizen militias instead of a professional standing army.

The problem was that the people's generosity was abused by having them fight senseless and unnecessary wars. And they rebelled (with the Vietnam War protests). So, instead of adapting their policy and limiting the military's role to one of defense, the government decided to develop career troops. "If you *choose* a military profession, then when war comes, you have no beef."

***

A key flaw in our educational approach is that almost all students are given the same general curriculum. Any variations are only in the levels of advancement.

There is no acknowledgment that different students have specialized talents and preferences. So our system gives the student body a broad but very superficial education.

After grade school, students could be interviewed and assessed, and placed in departments that focus on their aptitudes and/or stated preferences. Some choices would be: vocational, technical, police-military, legal, business, scientific, artistic, political, and athletic.

I would limit the mandatory classes to a few core life skills: public speaking, self-defense, basic logic and semantics.

I believe students would be more inspired and empowered by such an approach, instead of the more generic and impersonal one we have grown used to.

***

After school and all through the summer, life is often empty and boring for many kids. Their minds are idle. Gangs have unfortunately taken up the slack, utilizing kids' needs for solidarity and fitting in. But what if every city had positive youth gangs—privately or publicly sponsored—where kids could hang out, belong, and do interesting pro-active things like building projects, sports, field trips, community service and skills training? They could be like militias, where each group has its own name and wears its own "colors" (jackets or caps with distinctive insignia and decorations). That could be time well spent, which would likely make a difference during those formative years.

***

Anyone who thinks Lady Gaga looks like a dude sure has some funny ideas about what a dude looks like.

***

When government begins protecting the people from themselves, it assumes the stance of the people's owner. If it didn't consider itself the people's owner, it would never need to come between them and their own selves. The dynamic is similar to a rancher who takes care of his animals because it's in his interest that they be healthy.

***

One could argue that taxes and many government programs are only necessary because we have gotten so used to them; in the same way that, to a smoker, cigarettes appear so necessary.

***

Democrats and Republicans are both federalist parties. There wouldn't be much point to a major third party unless it was anti-federalist.

***

Patriotism isn't always just about "love of country." Some patriots are assholes about their love of country. They're in your face about it. All the chest-thumping, bravado, and flag-waving: so much *emotion!* It all reeks of overcompensation. Makes me suspect that, deep down, these patriots don't love their country so much as their *idea* of it.

But if you really love your country, you can go ahead and love it without having to prove anything to anybody.

***

Truth is, capitalism is *not* about having free markets. It's about having power and control over markets. Market dominance.

Free markets are the bane of capitalism. If you were a captain of industry, would *you* want more competition? Capitalism promotes the interests of industry captains, not consumers.

***

The Republican plan to lower spending makes me laugh by how silly and ineffective it is.

It's the equivalent of trying to save money by clipping supermarket coupons while deciding to buy two Porsches and three Ferraris.

Until deep cuts are made in the defense budget, it's all talk and no walk, GOP!

***

This Amanda Knox chick looks guilty as sin. Of course, that doesn't necessarily mean she is. But, no matter what faces she pulls, she always looks like the cat who swallowed the canary.

***

In the US, there is some popular contempt toward the French. I think it goes back to WW2 and how they quickly surrendered to Germany. This earned them a reputation for cowardice. But most people don't know that if the French resistance— four years later—hadn't thwarted the SS panzer divisions approaching Normandy from southern France, the Allies' toehold on the beaches would've

been blasted away. So I'd say the resistance re-
deemed the French with that one.

***

The odd thing about patriots in the USA is that
they often rail against the federal government. This
is odd because it's the federal government that con-
stitutes the United States of America—without it,
the USA would just be some other land. Before the
federal government took over, what is now the USA
was Native American, Spanish, French, English, and
Russian lands.

Say you're on the Canadian-USA border. What is
the difference between Canada and the USA? The
land itself looks pretty much the same. The difference is that the USA is the land the US federal government has jurisdiction over. That's it.

***

It shouldn't be a question of being against the
federal government but of improving how it func-
tions. The same goes for state, county, and city government. If government ably represents the people's interests (as it's mandated to do), it will have
the people's support. But, for that to happen, all the
clogging and choking special interests need to be
exorcized.

And by "representing the people's interests," I

don't mean a welfare nanny state; rather, a state that, where special interests and the people's well-being don't coincide, the state opts to support the latter.

***

A new trend in business is "the jobless need not apply."

Instead of giving jobs to the unemployed, you simply hire people who *already* have jobs.

Oh, this is simply brilliant. Great way to reduce unemployment!

***

The supposed "secret recipe" for Coca-Cola was published in the media yesterday. I was surprised that kola nut wasn't included, as I had always understood it was a key ingredient, along with the coca leaves extract. But the telltale sign that the recipe is fake is that high fructose corn syrup also wasn't included; instead it listed this thing called "sugar."

***

What can one make of Glenn Beck and John Boehner's crying jags? Each time one of them cries, it seems he's saying, "Me! Me! Me!"

***

If I believed what Republican politicians said, I'd be a Republican myself. But 80% of it is such a steaming pile of dissembling horse shit that I'm astounded at the gullibility of most Republican voters.

***

Sanctimonious dogmatic liberals are irritating. It's like they're attempting murder by "killing you with kindness." The paradox is that they're open-minded in a close-minded way.

***

There is something touching about how Republicans use logic and then consider it to be "the Truth."

***

I've often wondered, How would Dick Cheney respond to being given 700 micrograms of LSD and left in the middle of California's redwood forest for a couple days?

***

The crux of the Second Amendment is anti-militarism. The Founding Fathers had a lot to say about the dangers of "standing armies." Quick, someone notify Congress and the President.

***

"Department of Defense" is such a misnomer. It was more frankly named when it was called the War Department. George Orwell has been so consistently prescient.

***

For at least several years now, the advertising industry—especially on TV—has often taken to making Caucasian-Americans look like uncool fools vis-a-vis African-Americans. I suspect this is a response to hip hop's popularity. But what's going to happen if country music overtakes it?

***

The new FCC rules for net neutrality require that broadband providers let *all* subscribers access *all* legal online content, services and applications over their wired networks.

The Republicans are for the broadband providers and the Democrats are for the subscribers.

Note to internet users: Pick whichever side you

favor more.

***

Sometimes the government has to police the market for it to be free, just like on the streets there needs to be a police presence for the people to have their basic freedom and safety.

Without this government role, the corporations in each industry could band together and have their way with consumers, fixing prices and controlling information. Similarly, without a police role, gangs and crime syndicates could form a black market economy with exorbitant prices for needed goods ... and there wouldn't be a damn thing you could do about it.

***

Remember when Kanye West interrupted Taylor Swift at the VMAs to announce that Beyoncé's "Single Ladies" video was "one of the best videos of all time"? At that very instant, he showed the world how his taste in videos is really gay.

***

I'm not saying government should pamper and mollycoddle the people. I'm not even saying government should take care of the people. What I am saying is that government should refrain from colluding with special interests to work against the people. Without doubt, it owes the people at least that much.

**

The key problem with relying on the private sector to put up a social safety net is that the private sector is defined by its profit motive. If something is necessary and important to society but there's no money in it, it may never get accomplished.

**

With the Bush-Obama bailouts, socialism came to capitalism's rescue. This prevented the rising up of a stronger and smarter capitalism. Without death, there is no resurrection.

**

As a guitar player and performer in the '70s, Ted Nugent was riveting and fun. But as a political activist, he is a snooze fest. Why is that? Anything he had to say, he said better with rock 'n' roll and funny rock-star-attitude interviews, not aggro preaching. If you're a musician and can't or won't let the music do the talking, then maybe something is wrong.

***

I understand that growing up the Nuge was more inspired by Chuck Berry and Keith Richards than by Richard Nixon and Barry Goldwater.

***

The big secret in the USA is that socialism and capitalism are best friends forever, each enabling the other. The conflicts between the two are political theater, to make it "look good." Mixed economy, indeed. Each side has an arch-enemy (partner). It's a brilliant, two-pronged attack. A pincer movement. Divide and conquer.

In a sense it's not too surprising. Each system is, in its own way, obsessed with money. Power is power: whether it's public or private ... well, who cares? At the highest, most elite levels it makes no difference.

***

An economy where the wealthy get wealthier and the poor get poorer is imbalanced and therefore unstable and thus in danger of collapse.

If the wealthy were smart, they'd see themselves as part of the whole. And they'd be less predatory. But overall they're not smart. I'd say they're more cunning, which is different (intelligence applied only to short-term self-gain).

***

Republican leaders of yesteryear were often intellectual and eloquent. But they have gradually been usurped by products of the Dangerous Clown Syndrome.

Dolts who mock public service in the nation's highest levels by their very presence.

It began with Dan Quayle and peaked with George W. Bush.

***

Coca-Cola ... high fructose corn syrup, carbonated water, caffeine, phosphoric acid, and caramel coloring.

Quite a concoction!

***

We have a legal mass-market depressant (alcohol) and stimulant (caffeine). For balance, we need a comparable psychedelic.

***

It's almost as though the word "congressmen" could be shortened to "conmen."

***

The Triune Mind model states that people have three minds in one: the *neo-mammalian* is responsible for language, abstraction, planning, and perception; the *paleo-mammalian* for the motivation and emotion involved in social, nurturing and parental behaviors; and the *reptilian* for instinctual acts such as aggression, dominance, territoriality, and ritual displays. Everyone uses all three minds, and the neo-mammalian distinguishes us from other animals. But could it be that one of the differences between liberals and conservatives is that one group tends to emphasize the paleo-mammalian mind while the other emphasizes the reptilian? And, if so, do you want to guess who does which?

***

The three minds correspond to the Triune Brain model of neurology: neo-mammalian *(neocortex)*, paleo-mammalian *(limbic system)*, and reptilian *(basal ganglia)*. Some writers have pointed out that the three minds also respectively parallel other trinities from psychology and culture: thinking, feeling, and willing; head, heart, and gut; and, as in L. Frank Baum's fable *The Wizard of Oz,* a brain, a heart, and courage.

Applying this model to politics, one might conclude that conservatives are heartless, liberals are gutless, and both are brainless.

**

It's completely consistent with their respective ideologies that private Fox News is the Republican broadcasting center and public NPR the Democratic one.

**

I would like to see private non-profit health and vitality centers in every city and town. Safe havens open 24/7 where people could come in and spend some time, even up to a few weeks if necessary, and get alternative treatments, including massage therapy, rolfing, detoxification, purification, exercise, diet, counseling, check-ups, and so on. The environment would be clean and neat, comfortable and secure.

**

A lot of government spending amounts to investing in society, people, and jobs. Now everyone says we need to reduce government spending and I agree.

But which kind of spending are they referring to? Investing or wasting?

***

That fascism is left-wing is a distinctly conservative viewpoint—just like fascism being right-wing is a liberal viewpoint.

Fascism actually featured left- and right-wing elements. Today, this often does not compute with either conservatives or liberals.

***

Many Mexican immigrants work really hard. They have been toughened, kind of like Americans were during the 1930s.

But look at Rush Limbaugh and Mitch McConnell ... think those guys could ever do some hard physical work for more than, say, twenty minutes?

***

Technically, in order to love America as it is, you have to love every square inch of American land from the Grand Canyon to the worst ghetto, and love every single American citizen.

Otherwise you don't really love America as a whole, but just the America you agree with.

***

Pennies got to go. Screw the 100-cent pricing

strategy. Go find a new strategy.

A penny today is worth like 1/35th of a penny in the 1940s.

***

Giving corporations the same legal status as persons is something an asshole does.

***

The bankers' and the government's imposing income tax without the people's vote in 1913 was a joke. The death blow to the American Revolution. Even when the revolutionaries fought "taxation without representation," there was no such thing as income tax.

***

If Gadhaffi defeats the rebels, it could mean the Libyan people don't hate him enough. He's a bad guy but not "that bad." Not worth fighting or dying over. Ah, but the US and UN have a plan....

***

In his book *Liberal Fascism,* Jonah Goldberg tries to show how liberalism (including today's Democrats) is a form of fascism. He describes fascism several times as "right-wing socialism" and I agree with this description. But the reason why a lot of his book is so off is that it could just as well be titled *Liberal Right-Wing Socialism,* which really doesn't make much sense.

Unless, of course, you're including the Republican Party along with the Democratic Party.

***

I concur with Goldberg's basic premise that fascism doesn't have to be "evil" or "Hitlerian," that it can also be warm, friendly and well-intentioned.

***

In *Liberal Fascism,* Goldberg informs us that the fasces (the ancient Roman symbol adopted by Mussolini) is a "socialist symbol." I suppose he just couldn't resist. I'd say this one statement is a microcosm of the book as a whole.

***

Us Americans have gotten cushy and spoiled.

When gas hits $4 a gallon, everyone freaks. In most of the world, they've been paying $5 or more for years.

When unemployment here hits 10% ... people's heads spin. Again, so many countries for years have had 15% or higher.

***

In a nutshell, fascism can be defined as militaristic socialist populist capitalist nationalist statism.

If any one of these elements is missing, it's not fascism.

***

I wouldn't be surprised if Saudi Arabia at some point becomes simply Arabia again.

***

Truth is, even if we were to exploit all our resources and drill baby drill, we just don't have that much oil.

***

The tsunami and earthquake in Japan are a massive wake-up call that the consequences of pursuing nuclear power are too dangerous to contemplate. You're going to place nuclear energy and radioactive waste with a 10,000-year half-life right in between human error and the forces of nature? That's optimism gone out of bounds.

***

Yemen's prez Saleh could easily prevent civil war by just stepping down. But he doesn't want to. He thinks it should keep being about him. Step aside, sonny. Get out of the way. Somewhere along the line, you forgot you're just the chief public servant. That's all.

This happens with politicians all over, including in the USA. They think it's all about them and their careers and setting themselves up to make good money. It's not. You are in office to serve the public. Nothing more, nothing less.

It's about your role, your function. You yourself are extremely expendable.

***

Government should protect people from predators. Whether these take the form of street thugs, terrorists, top corporations, or foreign armies makes no difference.

***

Government only protecting you from others, not from yourself. No interference with self-liberty—your right to do whatever you want, including to yourself, so long as it doesn't imperil or harm someone else.

***

As far as having basic social services and a safety net, I think it's common sense, to a point. Why reinvent the wheel every five minutes? Anyway, if you're going to collect income tax, give the people a little something in return. Or are we going to be stingy about it?

None of these services would be mandatory. Just available for those who want them.

***

Jonah Goldberg equates unity or union with socialism/fascism. "Collectivism over individualism" and all that. I wonder what he makes of our country's name, the *United* States of America?

***

I've determined there are no "bad" groups. The villains are not blacks or Jews, whites or Hispanics. As disappointing as this may sound, it's not the rich or the poor, the bankers or the welfare recipients. Nor is it the conservatives or liberals, communists or fascists, Christians or Muslims. It's not even the lawyers, politicians, union members, fundamentalists, atheists, materialists or any other group. There are decent people in all these groups.

The true "villains" belong to every single one of

these groups and in fact are in every known group on earth, from the biggest to the smallest. But they haven't formed their own specific group. I refer to the assholes. They are the ones who cause most of the trouble—always have, always will. An asshole is a person who promotes his or her interests to the detriment of others. Wherever trouble is being caused, you'll find an asshole there, responsible for orchestrating it in some way. Of course, he or she usually won't call it "trouble" but something positive- or even noble-sounding.

***

In Spanish there's a saying, *"Pueblo chico, infierno grande."* Small town, big hell. In a small town everyone knows and judges you, and you have no privacy. Other people's bullshit becomes a part of your life too, whether you like it or not.

Because of the rapid developments in communications and technology, the world is becoming like a massive small town.

***

I wonder if statism (big government) is a product of industrial-technological evolution since this makes it easier to influence and manage more things across larger areas. Old barriers of time and space mean less and less. If so, then the tide of time could be going against true conservatives (libertarians). While authoritarian regimes date back to antiquity, I find it telling that statism (e.g. fascism, socialism and progressivism) didn't manifest until the early 20th century. But then again, statism itself was a response to capitalism, which appeared during the late 19th century (after the Industrial Revolution).

At any rate, if tech development by its very nature facilitates statism, then small-government conservatism is doomed.

***

The French Revolutionary regime was an early pioneer of statism but naturally couldn't implement the later capitalist inventions of scales of mass production and information. In this respect, then, it can't be considered "statist" in the modern sense.

***

President Obama got Osama bin Laden. That's all there is to it. The POTUS always gets the credit when these things go right, and the blame when they go wrong.

***

Newt Gingrich going into the 2012 election is like Hillary Clinton in 2008: a candidate very much of the '90s.

***

Yesterday, Rick Santorum told an interviewer that John McCain "doesn't understand" how enhanced interrogation works.

The problem with dumb people like Rick Santorum is that they're too dumb to realize how dumb they are.

***

I suspect that people who are passionately committed to either left- or right-wing platforms get many of their cues about what to think in reaction to what the other side thinks. At least in part. It's a sort of dance. It just seems remarkable that both groups would incidentally pick the exactly opposite positions on dozens of different issues.

***

Gadhaffi. Pirates. Anarchy. Sometimes I think things were better when Libya and Somalia were Italian colonies.

***

To call people "black" or "white" heightens the contrast between the races and is oppositional. It's more accurate to say that all people are different shades of brown, from light to dark. This indicates their commonality. "Black" and "white" are a fallacy. You'd never call a mixed-race person "grey."

***

With friends like Fannie Mae, Freddie Mac, and Sallie Mae, you really don't need any enemies. Sallie Mae, especially, is a total bitch.

***

Regarding human history, my theory is that life has always been exactly like it is right now, except that the fashions and technology have changed.

***

One thing the Iraq War and the TARP bailouts taught me is that the "perfect crime" is simply the legal crime.

www.ingramcontent.com/pod-product-compliance
Lightning Source LLC
Chambersburg PA
CBHW060637280326
41933CB00012B/2071